Patient Endurance

365 Days of Spiritual Motivation

Jennifer Le Blanc

ISBN 978-1-64349-489-0 (paperback)
ISBN 978-1-64349-490-6 (digital)

Copyright © 2018 by Jennifer Le Blanc

All rights reserved. No part of this publication may be reproduced, distributed, or transmitted in any form or by any means, including photocopying, recording, or other electronic or mechanical methods without the prior written permission of the publisher. For permission requests, solicit the publisher via the address below.

Christian Faith Publishing, Inc.
832 Park Avenue
Meadville, PA 16335
www.christianfaithpublishing.com

Scriptures are cited from the New Living Translation, unless otherwise noted. Original messages are without citation.

Printed in the United States of America

Unless otherwise indicated, all Scripture quotations are taken from the *Holy Bible,* New Living Translation, copyright © 1996, 2004, 2007, 2013 by Tyndale House Foundation. Used by permission of Tyndale House Publishers, Inc., Carol Stream, Illinois 60188. All rights reserved.

Scripture quotations marked (MSG) are taken from *THE MESSAGE.* Copyright © by Eugene H. Peterson 1993, 1994, 1995, 1996, 2000, 2001, 2002. Used by permission of NavPress. All rights reserved. Represented by Tyndale House Publishers, Inc.

Scripture quotations in this publication marked (CEB) are from the Common English Bible. © Copyright 2011 by the Common English Bible. All rights reserved. Used by permission.

Scripture quotations marked (CEV) are from the Contemporary English Version, Second Edition (CEV®) © 2006 American Bible Society. Used by Permission.

Bible text from the Contemporary English Version (CEV) is not to be reproduced in copies or otherwise by any means except as permitted in writing by American Bible Society, 101 North Independence Mall East, Floor 8, Philadelphia, PA 19106-2155 (www.americanbible.org).

Scripture quotations marked (TLV) are taken from the Tree of Life Translation of the Bible. Copyright © 2015 by The Messianic Jewish Family Bible Society. Used with permission.

Scriptures and additional materials marked as (GNB) are from the Good News Bible © 1994 published by the Bible Societies/HarperCollins Publishers Ltd UK, Good News Bible© American Bible Society 1966, 1971, 1976, 1992. Used with permission.

Cover photo taken by Iftekhar Uddin, MBBS, MSPH. Used with permission.

~ ~ ~

With sincere gratitude to God, my incredibly amazing and supportive family, my courageous physician, and to everyone who has supported me over the years. There is no way that I could have ever done this on my own. Thank you for saving my life and for helping me reach my life's purpose.

~ ~ ~

To everyone who has fought for their life or is still in the battle, you are thought of today. Though friends or family may have forgotten your illness or circumstance because you seem all well and fine, you are remembered today. We are made stronger through our battles, made better human beings with a greater amount of compassion . . . so keep fighting and know that you are not forgotten.

Remembering Courtney Jaclyn Levee

February 23, 1983–May 24, 2015

A letter to Cheryl and Joel Levee:

One morning in the month of October 2009, Courtney and I were lying awake in our Tennessee log cabin bed. You guys were going out into town to pick something up, and Courtney and I decided we were going to sleep in a little more. Eventually, we got around to waking up before you returned to the cabin. Of course, we had turned into seven-year-old children at that point and thought it would be absolutely hilarious to make it seem like we were still in bed when you guys got back. So, ever so thoughtfully, we positioned the pillows in such a way that it looked like we were still very well asleep. We heard you pull up and started giggling uncontrollably as we hid on the side of the bed. Joel walked in, took a peek in the room, and proclaimed, "Are you guys still in bed? You've got to be kidding me!" Courtney and I just could not contain ourselves anymore. Absolutely cracking up, we popped up from beside the bed . . . Surprise!

I think from all the memories that I have with Courtney, that one is definitely my favorite—being twenty-something years old and allowing our inner child to run around for a while. Then again, that's how it was with Courtney. She had such a joyful spirit and just wanted to live life in the most abundant way that she possibly could. She loved her family and her friends. With Courtney, you could always tell that she sincerely cherished every moment that she spent with you and others that she loved. I just thought of New Year's Eve back in 2007, where a whole bunch of us went to Howl at the Moon in Ft. Lauderdale. Man, Courtney's eyes were so bright that night that she alone could have lit up that whole place.

She always demonstrated what it means to live. That is, enjoy the smaller things because they actually turn out to be the really big things. Courtney knew what is really important in life. She had mastered the art of embracing the moment, cherishing every opportunity to go on a new adventure, spending time with friends, and getting a new tattoo. See, Courtney went to a school that most people never attend. Most people never attend this particular school because . . . well . . . quite honestly, it's only for the strongest, most badass people who are born on earth. The majority of people could not handle the intense training that Courtney underwent for thirty-two years. Simply put, most people are just not qualified to be Courtney.

Nevertheless, Courtney's battle was a real one. It was a battle that is incomprehensible to anyone outside of her body. Those that understand her fight the greatest are you and others with AT. You, who (in an understatement) were there for her from morning to morning. And you, who showed her the greatest definition of unconditional love.

Disease is stupid. Disease is cruel. Regardless of its type, it often forces a person to fight beyond their conceived limits. Not only does it affect its victim so greatly, but it often leaves that person's loved ones virtually helpless. Sometimes all a family member or friend can do is be there, listen to them, help them into a chair, feed them, or brush their hair. And while there can be some biological or physiological explanation to certain pathology, the real reason as to why certain people get different levels of disease—or any disease at all—remains a mystery. All that I have is the remaining thought that you have to have the strength of a true warrior to have something like AT.

We have all experienced a loss with Courtney's leaving of her body. And though we mourn for the loss that we feel, we must turn to all that she has gained. Courtney is no longer trapped within that body that kept her torturously trapped.

I had originally wanted to mention that Courtney is now resting in peace, free from her AT body. But really, who would I be kidding? We all know that Courtney is raising all kinds of craziness, right this very moment, partying it up like she always dreamed of doing. Courtney was a wild child while she took temporary residence here on earth. She was a sarcastic smart aleck with a sense of humor and a huge heart. There is no doubt that she is still all these things in her new place of residence, only now she does not have to experience the frustration of her body's limitations. And for that, we should be grateful and be filled with happiness for her.

I can't even imagine the true amazement and wonder that she felt those few days ago. I'm sure the word *freedom* does not even come close to the sensation that her spirit felt as she entered a place where there is an overabundance of joy and absolutely anything is possible. Never again will Courtney be trapped. Never again will she have to dream. Courtney is officially cured. No longer will ataxia telangiectasia or acute myelogenous leukemia be a heavy burden. And while the silence and her absence may be deafening, let us remember where she is now and how she must feel this very moment.

We may never have an understanding for why Courtney was given such a difficult road. What we do know is that she did a damn good job at traveling it. And while we may never understand why Mariah Carey was her selected soundtrack, what we do know is that Courtney was a sincere woman who cherished each person in her life and each moment she was given. She will be missed dearly here on earth, but she is now being treasured in heaven. I wonder if she's had orientation yet.

Patient Endurance:
A Brief Story of How It Began

Does it ever feel as though your patience is constantly being tested? Have you ever wondered why your prayers seem to be taking so long to be answered? I surely know that I have experienced these things. For over twenty years, I fought a battle with Lyme Borreliosis Complex (LBC), a multisystemic, multiorganism, complex, infectious disease. I did not know that this is what I had been living with until I was twenty-two years old, at which point I had gone undiagnosed by numerous doctors for fifteen years. From joint and muscle pain to severe fatigue, brain fog, loss of vision, and difficulty walking and speaking, no doctor could figure it out.

When I finally received an answer as to why I had been feeling these things for so many years, I thought that life would now become easier with treatment. However, I was soon to learn the test that is patient endurance. Lyme Borreliosis Complex is amid a horrible controversy that has allowed for great suffering for millions of people worldwide. I have seen the many devastating stories that others have with this disease. I have also seen people enter remission for years. I often wondered why it was taking me so long to recover, particularly when I would see so many others finding healing so much faster than what I had observed for myself. I prayed and trusted that I would have been rid of this thing or in remission—by now. However, I remained in a very active battle with a disease that affected every aspect of my body.

I have finally learned to appreciate the "fortunately unfortunate" situation that I have been entrusted with. As I began the work on this book, I was miraculously finishing my second year of medical school. I was constantly reminded of what it felt like to be a chronically ill patient. With much ignorance surrounding me, I felt humiliated on a few occasions for having a disease that everyone is at risk for.

I waited patiently for my total healing to come, healing where I may feel "normal" and without pain or mental anguish. However, I knew that the lessons I was learning could come no other way. If I were to be a true physician, I must be able to appreciate what my patients experience from one day to the next. Indeed, I have been fortunately unfortunate to have Lyme. How many doctors can appreciate such things? I have learned so many life lessons, and I have become stronger than I ever could have, had I not been so sick.

I have been blessed with an incredibly amazing and supportive family, who has been there for me every step of my journey. Not only was I blessed to have been diagnosed at all, but I was blessed to have the best Lyme physician anyone could ever ask for, one who is an example of what living for God truly looks like.

I know that God is using my experience with this disease and the many detours of my life to remind me of what is important and what it is I am to do here on this earth. You see, while I was undiagnosed, I was pursuing a career as a physician. I ended up going to a medical school abroad, where financial aid was strongly lacking. The school had promised the students that they would be approved for US federal loans in the upcoming semester or two, so the students held onto that hope. In the meantime, many of us began working on a master's degree simultaneously, where we could receive funds for the master's program and living expenses. As the semesters passed by, my medical school continued to mislead the students. As the students found out, from our own investigations, the school had withdrawn their Title IV application to the Department of Education the year prior and had never resubmitted another one. By this point, there was no possible way for me to stay at this school, having nearly maxed out on credit cards to pay for food and no other means of income.

I decided to transfer to another school, where private loans were available, given you had a minimum credit score. Initially, my score was not high enough, so I got a job at a mall and anticipated starting this new school in a few months. I booked the flight and made arrangements. As the months went by, my credit score still had not increased to the minimum score. Then suddenly, just before I was supposed to leave, my credit raised to a score higher than what was needed. I could now continue my medical education.

After finishing my basic science courses, I studied for the United States Medical Licensing Exam Step 1 and passed. I was then placed into clinical rotations in Baltimore, Maryland (a place where I swore I would never return). I completed four rotations and graduated from my master's program when my credit score dropped again. I could no longer obtain the private loans to continue. Family members helped as best as they could, but in October of 2014, the cost of tuition was simply too great.

At the time that I lost funding for medical school, the road of my next detour had already been paved. When I was doing my rotations in Baltimore in 2013, the director of my rotations had us going to grand rounds at Johns Hopkins Hospital. He himself had been a cardiothoracic surgeon there and projected such respect for the school. One day, a colleague and I went to the bookstore of the medical campus after grand rounds. I wondered if Hopkins had any sort of part-time master's programs that were available, so I went home and did some research. As it turns out, the school of public health offered a master's degree, which could be completed as a part time student.

Given that they are the number-one school of public health, I thought that my chances of getting in were literally impossible. Nevertheless, I became inspired and anticipated applying to the program. I bought a sweatshirt and sweatpants with the Hopkins name. Of course, I felt like a phony whenever I wore them. This was particularly true when I wore the sweatshirt on a plane and was asked, "Do you go to Hopkins?" After watching a sermon by John Maxwell at my church back home, I decided to walk around the Bloomberg School of Public Health after the next grand rounds and declare acceptance as mine. So that is indeed what I did. I walked around the entire building and said out loud, "I declare acceptance to this school in Jesus's name." I then went back over to the bookstore and bought a decal with the school's name on it. Each day, I would stand on it and say out loud, "I declare acceptance to this school in Jesus's name." I said it would be a literal miracle if I were accepted, particularly since I opted against taking the GRE. I received letters of recommendation from three academic physicians and used birthday money from my godparents to pay for the application fees.

After my transcripts were lost several times and the application process changed, I began to have doubts. After some motherly encouragement, I applied and received my acceptance in September of 2014, one month before I would find out that medical school would be put on hold once more. I began applying to jobs across the country, totaling over two thousand. I moved out west to stay with my sister and brother-in-law, hoping to find a job that would help pay the loans that were in repayment and to hopefully save up enough money to finish my last semester of medical school.

After getting jobs as a hostess and sales associate, I soon began to lose myself and any sense of purpose. I was not making enough money to set some aside. I felt as though I was not where I was supposed to be. Baltimore had treated me well, and I felt that perhaps that was where I was supposed to return. Confirmation from a Hillsong sermon, an amazing hair dresser, and my mom and sister motivated me to make a bold move. I packed my bags from California, picked up the car that my aunt and uncle were letting me use back home, and drove it to Baltimore. I didn't have a job or apartment in Baltimore. I just knew that that was where I was supposed to go. Two friends offered for me to stay with them while I searched for a job. Within one week of being back in Maryland, I had a job at the Hopkins bookstore and a place to live. A year and a half later, I met the man I would marry.

At Johns Hopkins, I received a small scholarship and enough money to attend two courses per term. This put me at the school for two and a half years, where I was able to concentrate my degree in Infectious Diseases, while also obtaining a certificate in Global Health. During my time there, I worked as a research assistant for the School of Public Health and for the School of Medicine. I was introduced to several different areas of public health and participated in several different research projects. I also worked at the school's bookstore on weekends while still searching for jobs to help pay bills and medical school.

There are many pieces of this story that have not been mentioned, but this is the general overview of the past few years of my life. Throughout these years, I have faced many struggles, much doubt, and times of great despair. I have been blessed with encouraging family members and genuine friends. I have met some incredibly strong and courageous people; some of whom have quite literally saved my life. Through my experience with great financial struggles, being a survivor of a sexual predator, and my battle with LBC, I know that I am being transformed into the woman I need to become to help those around me. Despite my times of doubt, I always fall back on my faith in God. Without Him, I don't know where I would be today. I still don't know what the future holds for my life, but at this point, I know that I truly do not have control. All I can do is let go and continue on the road that He has designed, whether I understand it or not.

This book is a collection of scriptures that have spoken to me and reinforced strength and courage to continue on in this fight. It is also a collection of my own thoughts, prayers, and messages. I pray that each message brings you strength and courage as you press on with patient endurance for the will that God has planned for you and your life.

Day 1

Endurance.
It is made through our difficult moments, made through our difficult times. Patient endurance is waiting with faith, knowing that as we press on through those difficult moments, the Lord is with us always. And knowing this, we may be patient, waiting for His perfect timing.

Day 2

"Never stop praying" (1 Thessalonians 5:17).

This one seems like a rather "common sense" approach to life, but I know that I have been guilty of praying to God when I felt I needed something especially greater at a few separate times. However, we need him always. Regardless of our situation, be it a struggle or a glorious moment, we need Him. Prayer is our great communication with Him.

And while we may tend to ask Him for things rather often, let us not forget to thank him and glorify Him. Prayer is the way to let him know what you need and what you are grateful for.

Day 3

"In his kindness, God called you to share in his eternal glory by means of Christ Jesus. So after you have suffered a little while, he will restore, support, and strengthen you, and he will place you on a firm foundation" (1 Peter 5:10).

Day 4

Sometimes our faith is tested more than we care to ever even imagine. We have to always remember that no matter what our circumstance, He will always provide and pull through for us. Even if it is until that final hour, He will solve our problem, give us a way out, and restore our hope.

Day 5

"Whatever was written in the past was written for our instruction so that we could have hope through endurance and through the encouragement of the scriptures" (Romans 15:4 CEB).

Let us follow the instructions of the Word of God so that we may live the life we were made to live.

Day 6

"But all of you who were faithful to the Lord your God are still alive today—every one of you" (Deuteronomy 4:4 NLT).

Day 7

In your weakness, He is strong. Keep your faith firmly grounded in Him and his promises. Remain faithful to Him and He will not fail you. You will remain standing when this is through.

Day 8

"If you do this and God directs you, then you will be able to endure. And all these people will be able to go back to their homes much happier" (Exodus 18:23 CEB).

Day 9

He will give you the strength and courage needed to get through this. Do not be afraid because of your circumstance. Just know that there is an answer to whatever it is that you are going through.

Day 10

Whatever battle you are fighting through, you must keep your faith in Him. If that faith is the size of a mustard seed, it is enough for your battle to be won.

Day 11

"Dear friends, don't be surprised at the fiery trials you are going through as if something strange were happening to you. Instead, be very glad—for these trials make you partners with Christ in his suffering, so that you will have the wonderful joy of seeing his glory when it is revealed to all the world" (1 Peter 4:12–13).

Day 12

Let us remember today that our spirit is becoming physically fit for Jesus. While we may not be able to understand why we are going through what we go through, let us remember that He suffered greatly for us so that we may experience something greater. I know that I would like to be more like Jesus. And if this is what it takes, so be it.

Day 13

"That's why we ourselves are bragging about you in God's churches. We tell about your endurance and faithfulness in all the harassments and trouble that you have put up with" (2 Thessalonians 1:4 CEB).

Day 14

You may not realize what impact your faith has on those around you. For when the scriptures tell of the endurance and faithfulness through harassments and trouble, it illustrates what a firm believer looks like.

Let us be those firm believers, those with unfailing and unshakable faith. It is through such things that others will see that there is indeed something different about us: Jesus.

Day 15

"Patient people will hold themselves back until the right moment, and afterward they will be paid back with joy" (Sirach 1:23 CEB).

Day 16

How many times have you so desperately wanted to open your mouth or act upon a situation?

Sometimes we act or speak too soon, where if we just waited a few moments longer, we would have had a better result than if we rushed to the solution we thought we wanted. It may be difficult to wait a little longer, but not only do we build endurance in the waiting periods, but we set ourselves up to receive a greater solution.

Day 17

"Don't let anyone think less of you because you are young. Be an example to all believers in what you say, in the way you live, in your love, your faith, and your purity" (1 Timothy 4:12).

Day 18

Sometimes it can be discouraging when we are not taken seriously. Let us not feel inferior just because of someone else's thoughts or opinions. Just because we are different, young, or old, it does not mean we are lacking in our faith or spirit. Let us remember this so that we do not make ourselves into the person some may think of us to be.

Day 19

"All you who wait for the Lord, be strong and let your heart take courage" (Psalm 31:24 CEB).

Day 20

Be absolutely courageous.
What you are struggling with may indeed take some extra courage and a great deal of strength and endurance to keep going. Remember that He is still with you even if you are not feeling all too strong. Let Him be the source of your courage and strength. He will not let you down.

Day 21

"One said, 'Have courage, brother!' Another said, 'Keep going with honor'" (4 Maccabees 13:11 CEB).

Day 22

Keep your head held high, knowing that what you are doing is the right thing. Do not be dismayed by some of the lies that may be running around you. Keeping your head high and your eyes focused on the Lord, you will see the end of this.

Day 23

"If anyone loves to do what is right, laboring with Wisdom will produce every virtue. She trains persons to learn moderation and practical wisdom. She teaches them what is right and how to exercise courage. Nothing is more advantageous than these when it comes to human existence" (Wisdom of Solomon 8:7 CEB).

Day 24

Do what is right, know when to refrain
and when to carry on.

Day 25

When you stop fighting, you surrender
yourself to the fight.
When you keep fighting, you get stronger in it.
You soon become able to help others in their battles.

Day 26

"But the Lord is faithful; he will strengthen you and guard you from the evil one" (2 Thessalonians 3:3).

Day 27

We cannot forget that there is a force trying to hold us back from living out our purpose.

During the battles that we encounter, God will use the hard moments to help strengthen us so that we may become greater warriors for His cause. He will not allow us anything too great.

Day 28

"I know all the things you do. I have seen your love, your faith, your service, and your patient endurance. And I can see your constant improvement in all these things" (Revelation 2:19).

Day 29

He knows how hard you have been working and praying, and He does not want you to feel unnoticed. He is proud of you for your accomplishments.

Day 30

Why can't you have it all? If you are a follower of Christ, He will provide you with all that you need and desire. Follow the passion that he places within your heart and you will find peace.

Day 31

"I know all the things you do. I have seen your hard work and your patient endurance. I know you don't tolerate evil people. You have examined the claims of those who say they are apostles but are not. You have discovered they are liars" (Revelation 2:2).

Day 32

He has seen your heart and the patience that you have been building upon. He knows that you are frustrated. He knows that you cannot stand devastation and destruction. He knows that you fight against these things. Do not slow your endurance. You are doing the right things.

Day 33

I'm not sure that there is a more overwhelmingly amazing feeling than when you realize you have just changed someone's life.

Do something today for someone else. Do something greater than you could normally imagine to do.

Day 34

"You have patiently suffered for me without quitting" (Revelation 2:3).

Day 35

He knows what you have been through, as He has been with you every step of the way. He knows what heartache you have experienced, as He has watched you through these times. He has heard your prayers and heard your pleas. He knows that you have been waiting for the answers. And He knows that you have continued on despite the frustration and pain.

Day 36

"So humble yourselves under the mighty power of God, and at the right time he will lift you up in honor. Give all your worries and cares to God, for he cares about you" (1 Peter 5:6–7).

Day 37

Sometimes our goals may seem so large that they seem almost impossible to reach. Remember that nothing happens overnight. Those who achieve the greatest goals work consistently one step at a time.

Day 38

I know that it becomes so difficult sometimes to keep believing that the answer is coming. I know that what you are going through may be taking all that is within you to keep going. Let us remember that He does not give us more than we can handle. In His perfect timing, He will bring the answer to you. When you are having a hard time with this, surrender it all to Him. Let Him deal with this problem, for He is far greater a problem solver than us. Then He will reveal His answer in His perfect timing. You will go unharmed and with greater strength.

Day 39

Do not be afraid of being alone. For you are never truly alone in this life. I know that it may sometimes feel as though there is no one to turn to, but there is indeed the One. Sometimes He requires us to be alone with Him so that we may strengthen our spirit and so that we may know Him greater. Once we understand this, we may experience something greater than we could have ever imagined.

Day 40

"Stay alert! Watch out for your great enemy, the devil. He prowls around like a roaring lion, looking for someone to devour. Stand firm against him, and be strong in your faith. Remember that your Christian brothers and sisters all over the world are going through the same kind of suffering you are" (1 Peter 5:8–9).

Day 41

Indeed, there is a great enemy who wants nothing more than for you to give up or fail. Let us not let him win this battle. When you are in Christ Jesus, the enemy has no stronghold on you. Let us be able to recognize his lies and destruction that he may throw our way. We are strong because we are in Christ. And with Christ, we can do all things. There is nothing that we cannot do. And that includes defeating our enemies.

Day 42

To be a blessing to others is a blessing unto you.
So let yourself be blessed through the
good works you do for others.

Day 43

"God has given each of you a gift from his great variety of spiritual gifts. Use them well to serve one another. Do you have the gift of speaking? Then speak as though God himself were speaking through you. Do you have the gift of helping others? Do it with all the strength and energy that God supplies. Then everything you do will bring glory to God through Jesus Christ. All glory and power to him forever and ever! Amen" (1 Peter 4:10–11).

Day 44

Again, do not forget about the gifts that you have been given. You have been chosen to receive these gifts so that you may use them for His glory. If you are not sure about your gift, do not forget to pray about it. For the scriptures tell us to never stop praying. So let this be one of the things that you pray for. If you know your gift, do not be afraid to use it. It was given to you for a purpose. If you do not use it, how do you know that you will truly fulfill your whole purpose? It is important that you use the gifts that have been given to you.

Day 45

Why is it that again you find yourself doubting? How is it that you have not yet learned His love and promises? Don't you know that He wants what is best for you? Don't you know by now that he will never fail you? Wait patiently, my dear brothers and sisters in Christ. Wait with all that is within you. Remember that you are building the endurance needed for your purpose. This is all for a greater purpose than what you could ever imagine. So fear not and learn to trust in Him alone.

Day 46

"How do you know what your life will be like tomorrow? Your life is like the morning fog—it's here a little while, then it's gone. What you ought to say is, 'If the Lord wants us to, we will live and do this or that.' Otherwise, you are boasting about your own plans, and all such boasting is evil" (James 4:14–16).

Day 47

"So you see, faith by itself isn't enough. Unless it produces good deeds, it is dead and useless. So you see, we are shown to be right with God by what we do, not by faith alone" (James 2:17, 24).

Day 48

"And yet, better to have one handful with quietness than two handfuls with hard work and chasing the wind" (Ecclesiastes 4:6).

Day 49

So my dear brothers and sisters, build within you the fire that has been placed within your heart, the passion that stirs within your soul. You have been given these things so that your path may be guided according to His will for your life. For why else would you have such a desire to pursue such things? That is, of course, that you are pursuing the will of the Lord God and His purpose for your life. Do not pursue the foolish things of this earth. But always be reminded of the greater things that He has in store for you. As you endure these hardships, you are building upon the foundation of Christ. And surely such a foundation will never falter.

Day 50

For what you seek to achieve, you will achieve. It may take some time, which will require patience. But be reassured that your patient endurance is building so that you may be able to conquer your next adventure.

Day 51

Do not yourself try to answer the questions that only God can answer, nor try to solve the problems that only God can solve.

Day 52

Make your home a place of worship. For why should you wait for a Sunday to enter a place of worship? If God is within you, is He then not also in your home? Is your home not then the home of God also?

Day 53

"God blesses those who patiently endure testing and temptation. Afterward they will receive the crown of life that God has promised to those who love him" (James 1:12).

Day 54

Plant yourself in a strong church and allow your roots to gain firm ground. Your spirit will need this through your journey.

Day 55

"Don't love money; be satisfied with what you have. For God has said, 'I will never fail you. I will never abandon you'" (Hebrews 13:5).

Day 56

You have not failed at achieving your goals because you are not yet done with your journey. Do not stop working. Do not give up!

Day 57

"May he equip you with all you need for doing his will. May he produce in you, through the power of Jesus Christ, every good thing that is pleasing to him. All glory to him forever and ever! Amen" (Hebrews 13:21).

Day 58

"So take a new grip with your tired hands and strengthen your weak knees. Mark out a straight path for your feet so that those who are weak and lame will not fall but become strong" (Hebrews 12:12–13).

Day 59

"Faith is the confidence that what we hope for will actually happen; it gives us assurance about things we cannot see" (Hebrews 11:1).

Day 60

And it is through Him that this deep fire within me continues to grow greater than ever before. It is a roaring fire that is inextinguishable. It is a fire to fight for the sick and unheard, a fire to become greater at loving people and learning how to be a better human being. Through obedience to Him, He continues to provide one miraculous lesson after another, and so I will continue to serve His people so that I will continue to serve Him, showing His amazing love to all whose paths I cross.

Day 61

"Yes, and everyone who wants to live a godly life in Christ Jesus will suffer persecution" (2 Timothy 3:1).

Day 62

"A servant of the Lord must not quarrel but must be kind to everyone, be able to teach, and be patient with difficult people" (2 Timothy 2:24).

Day 63

Do not wait for justice to occur here on earth. You may or may not find it here. Trust me—I waited for quite a while for "justice" that never came. But I know that whatever injustice was done to me will be dealt with by Him. For He will not let such injustice go unnoticed. He will not let your suffering be left in vain.

Day 64

"Be strong through the grace that God gives you in Christ Jesus" (2 Timothy 2:1).

Day 65

"I thank Christ Jesus our Lord, who has given me strength to do his work. He considered me trustworthy and appointed me to serve him. Oh, how generous and gracious our Lord was! He filled me with the faith and love that comes from Christ Jesus" (1 Timothy 1:12, 14).

Day 66

"And we are confident in the Lord that you are doing and will continue to do the things we commanded you. May the Lord lead your hearts into a full understanding and expression of the love of God and the patient endurance that comes from Christ" (2 Thessalonians 3:4–5)

Day 67

"Now may the Lord of peace himself give you his peace at all times and in every situation. The Lord be with you all" (2 Thessalonians 3:16).

Day 68

"So we keep on praying for you, asking our God to enable you to live a life worthy of his call. May he give you the power to accomplish all the good things your faith prompts you to do" (2 Thessalonians 1:11).

Day 69

"Always be joyful" (1 Thessalonians 5:16).

Day 70

"Be thankful in all circumstances, for this is God's will for you who belong to Christ Jesus" (1 Thessalonians 5:18).

Day 71

"Let your roots grow down into him, and let your lives be built on him. Then your faith will grow strong in the truth you were taught, and you will overflow with thankfulness" (Colossians 2:7).

Day 72

"I don't mean to say that I have already achieved these things or that I have already reached perfection. But I press on to possess that perfection for which Christ Jesus first possessed me" (Philippians 3:12).

Day 73

"Let me hear of your unfailing love each morning, for I am trusting you. Show me where to walk, for I give myself to you" (Psalm 143:8).

Day 74

"Show me the right path, O Lord; point out the road for me to follow" (Psalm 25:4).

Day 75

"Don't worry about anything; instead, pray about everything. Tell God what you need, and thank him for all he has done. Then you will experience God's peace, which exceeds anything we can understand. His peace will guard your hearts and minds as you live in Christ Jesus" (Philippians 4:6–7)

Day 76

I know that you may be rather exhausted at this point. But know that it is at this moment that you will become closer to God. It is during these times that we need Him the most and where we may begin to see His works with our human eyes. It is sometimes easier to say that we cling to Him during the glorious times, but do we stray when we become weary? These are the moments where our patient endurance and faith are truly tested.

Day 77

"For God is working in you, giving you the desire and the power to do what pleases him" (Philippians 2:13).

Day 78

"There's an opportune time to do things, a right time for everything on the earth" (Ecclesiastes 3:1 MSG).

Day 79

"And I am certain that God who began the good work within you will continue his work until it is finally finished on the day when Christ Jesus returns" (Philippians 1:6).

Day 80

Whatever it is that you are facing, whatever it is that you are waiting for, never look away from our Lord Jesus Christ. Keep your eyes focused on Him during this trial. This not only keeps our focus where it should be, but it also helps battle the lies placed within our minds.

Day 81

"Be strong in the Lord and in his mighty power. Put on all of God's armor so that you will be able to stand firm against all strategies of the devil. For we are not fighting against flesh and blood enemies, but against evil rules and authorities of the unseen world, against mighty powers in this dark world, and against evil spirits in the heavenly places.

"Therefore, put on every piece of God's armor so you will be able to resist the enemy in the time of evil. Then after the battle you will still be standing firm. Stand your ground, putting on the belt of truth and the body armor of God's righteousness. For shoes, put on the peace that comes from the Good News so that you will be fully prepared. In addition to all of these, hold up the shield of faith to stop the fiery arrows of the devil. Put on salvation as your helmet, and take the sword of the Spirit, which is the word of God.

"Pray in the Spirit at all times and on every occasion. Stay alert and be persistent in your prayers for all believers everywhere" (Ephesians 6:10–18).

Day 82

"We are pressed on every side by troubles, but we are not crushed. We are perplexed, but not driven to despair. We are hunted down, but never abandoned by God. We get knocked down, but we are not destroyed" (2 Corinthians 4:8–9).

Day 83

"You're blessed when your commitment to God provokes persecution. The persecution drives you even deeper into God's kingdom" (Matthew 5:10 MSG).

Day 84

"For you have been given not only the privilege of trusting in Christ but also the privilege of suffering for him. We are in this struggle together. You have seen my struggle in the past, and you know that I am still in the midst of it" (Philippians 1:29–30).

Day 85

"All of this is for your benefit. And as God's grace reaches more and more people, there will be great thanksgiving, and God will receive more and more glory" (2 Corinthians 4:15).

Day 86

"That is why we never give up. Though our bodies are dying, our spirits are being renewed every day. For our present troubles are small and won't last very long. Yet they produce for us a glory that vastly outweighs them and will last forever!" (2 Corinthians 4:16–17).

Day 87

The only person stopping you is you.

Day 88

"So we don't look at the troubles we can see now; rather, we fix our gaze on things that cannot be seen. For the things we see now will soon be gone, but the things we cannot see will last forever" (2 Corinthians 4:18).

Day 89

"For we live by believing not seeing" (2 Corinthians 5:7).

Day 90

Tongues and Prophesy (1 Corinthians 14)

On July 20, 2013, at the *Amazing* conference at Christ Fellowship Church, I heard, "When the words come." I kept waiting for the rest of the sentence. *When the words come . . . what?* I kept thinking to myself. I was getting frustrated, thinking I was crazy or imagining this message I was receiving. It was only a small wait until I received the rest of the message. Nevertheless, I felt my patience being tested once again. It was the very next day during church service that I received the second half of the sentence.

That was my last weekend at my church for a while, as I was heading off to my clinical rotations for medical school. So that week, I was trying to absorb (or *stock up* should I say) all that I could before I ventured off.

Needless to say, God provides such amazing miracles to us when we completely and honestly surrender our whole being to Him.

During worship the next day, I received the full message: "When the words come, all will know that Jesus Christ is King." It was not more than even a few seconds that the gift of tongues was given to me. I honestly do not remember if it started as a thought or my whispering in tongues. All of a sudden though, the volume of my voice was turned up, and my spirit led to an exaltation in tongues during worship. I do not recall ever being so filled than at that moment. That was the first time I had ever spoken in tongues; and though I did not receive the translation, what a wondrous gift I was given- to communicate in such a sacred way with my spirit, to the Holy Spirit!

Day 91

"So my dear brothers and sisters, be strong and immovable, Always work enthusiastically for the Lord, for you know that nothing you do for the Lord is ever useless" (1 Corinthians 15:58).

Day 92

"The temptations in your life are no different from what others experience. And God is faithful. He will not allow the temptation to be more than you can stand. When you are tempted, he will show you a way out so that you can endure" (1 Corinthians 10:13).

Day 93

"God is our refuge and strength, a help always near in times of great trouble" (Psalm 46:1 CEB).

Day 94

Have you put your armor on today?

Day 95

The road to healing may be a long one, but do not ignore the lessons presented along that road.

Day 96

"But people who aren't spiritual can't receive these truths from God's Spirit. It all sounds foolish to them and they can't understand it, for only those who are spiritual can understand what the Spirit means" (1 Corinthians 2:14).

Day 97

Be patient, my dear brothers and sisters. I know that you are struggling. I know that you are frustrated. But be patient, knowing that He has something amazing planned for your life.

Day 98

"No, the wisdom we speak of is the mystery of God—his plan that was previously hidden, even though he made it for our ultimate glory before the world began. But the rulers of this world have not understood it; if they had, they would not have crucified our glorious Lord. That is what the Scriptures mean when they say, 'No eye has seen, no ear has heard, and no mind has imagined what God has prepared for those who love him'" (1 Corinthians 2:7–9).

Day 99

"The God of peace will soon crush satan under your feet. May the grace of our Lord Jesus be with you" (Romans 16:20).

Day 100

You can be given all the support and resources you need, but if you don't have the confidence or belief in yourself, none of that matters.

Day 101

"Yet I dare not boast about anything except what Christ has done through me, bringing the Gentiles to God by my message and by the way I worked among them" (Romans 15:18).

Day 102

Breaking a habit most surely requires patience. So be patient with yourself and know that with each passing day you are becoming stronger at overcoming this hardship. Do not give up on yourself because you are worth every good thing.

Day 103

"I pray that God, the source of hope, will fill you completely with joy and peace because you trust in him. Then you will overflow with confident hope through the power of the Holy Spirit" (Romans 15:13).

Day 104

When you speak of your faith, how do you do so?
Do you speak with conviction and confidence,
or do you speak with doubt in your heart?

Day 105

"Dear friends, never take revenge. Leave that to the righteous anger of God. For the Scriptures say, 'I will take revenge; I will pay them back,' says the Lord" (Romans 12:19).

Day 106

Do not be disheartened by the trials that you experience. Rather, hold on to God with a greater embrace than ever before. He will help you through this.

Day 107

"You're blessed when you feel you've lost what is most dear to you. Only then can you be embraced by the One most dear to you" (Matthew 5:4 MSG).

Day 108

"Don't let evil conquer you, but conquer evil by doing good" (Romans 12:21).

Day 109

Please realize that if you are experiencing something difficult, you do have a choice on how you deal with it. You can complain about it and remain bitter, or you can embrace the situation so that your endurance can grow. Let us not forget that everything is for a greater purpose. Complaining and being resentful or bitter only harms you. It prevents you from learning the lesson you are supposed to learn.

Day 110

"And we know that God causes everything to work together for the good of those who love God and are called according to his purpose for them" (Romans 8:28).

Day 111

"But if we look forward to something we don't yet have, we must wait patiently and confidently" (Romans 8:25).

Day 112

"We can rejoice, too, when we run into problems and trials, for we know that they help us develop endurance. And endurance develops strength of character, and character strengthens our confident hope of salvation. And this hope will not lead to disappointment. For we know how dearly God loves us, because he has given us the Holy Spirit to fill our hearts with his love" (Romans 5:3–5).

Day 113

"So the promise is received by faith" (Romans 4:16).

Day 114

"For I long to visit you so I can bring you some spiritual gift that will help you grow strong in the Lord" (Romans 1:11).

Day 115

The concept of patient endurance reminds me of working out. It takes a lot of time, sweat, and pain to get the body we aim to achieve. Such truth remains the same for other circumstances in our lives. But if we do not give up, we will achieve what God has planned for us.

Day 116

While many people have different definitions of success, the one truth remains: it doesn't happen by doing nothing.

Day 117

"When we get together, I want to encourage you in your faith, but I also want to be encouraged by yours" (Romans 1:12).

Day 118

"God says, 'At the time I have planned, I will bring justice against the wicked'" (Psalm 75:2).

Day 119

"Patient persistence pierces through indifference; gentle speech breaks down rigid defenses" (Proverbs 25:15 MSG).

Day 120

"But it won't work that way with the family of Israel. They won't listen to you because they won't listen to me. They are, as I said, a hard case, hardened in their sin. But I'll make you as hard in your way as they are in theirs. I'll make your face as hard as rock, harder than granite. Don't let them intimidate you. Don't be afraid of them, even though they're a bunch of rebels" (Ezekiel 3:7–9 MSG).

Day 121

"Finishing is better than starting. Patience is better than pride" (Ecclesiastes 7:8 NLT).

Day 122

I have observed that the most successful people have been through the most obstacles.

So if you find yourself going through hardship after hardship, take that as a sign that you have an incredible future ahead of you.

The key is you need to learn and grow from each struggle in order to become great.

Day 123

"Love is patient and kind. Love is not jealous or boastful or proud" (1 Corinthians 13:4).

Day 124

"But the Holy Spirit produces this kind of fruit in our lives: love, joy, peace, patience, kindness, goodness, faithfulness" (Galatians 5:22).

Day 125

Try not to become discouraged with how long this is taking. Remember that all things happen in His timing, according to His will. You are not behind not late nor early. You are right on time.

Day 126

"Always be humble and gentle. Be patient with each other, making allowance for each other's faults because of your love" (Ephesians 4:2).

Day 127

"This hope is like a firm and steady anchor for our souls. In fact, hope reaches behind the curtain and into the most holy place" (Hebrews 6:19 CEV).

Day 128

"The Lord took control of me and said, 'Stand up! Go into the valley and I will talk with you there'" (Ezekiel 3:22 CEV)

Day 129

If the people surrounding you are not helping you become a better you, go find new people and if you're not sure how to find new people, I will be more than happy to introduce you to some.

Day 130

"Wait patiently for the Lord. Be brave and courageous. Yes, wait patiently for the Lord" (Psalm 27:14).

Day 131

One of the great things about being exhausted is that this is where we may become closer than ever to God. These moments provide the opportunity to build our faith, our strength, and our spiritual endurance.

Day 132

"The Lord is my light and my salvation—so why should I be afraid?" (Psalm 27:1 NLT).

Day 133

"Then Jesus said, 'Come to me, all of you who are weary and carry heavy burdens, and I will give you rest'" (Matthew 11:28 NLT).

Day 134

That day when you realize you could have been there by now, don't let it happen. Change the way you think right now and change your life. Then you'll wake up on that same day and instead say, "Wow, look at how much I have accomplished because I decided I was worth it!"

Day 135

"Avoid stupid controversies, genealogies, and fights about the Law, because they are useless and worthless. After a first and second warning, have nothing more to do with a person who causes conflict, because you know that someone like this is twisted and sinful—so they condemn themselves" (Titus 3:9–11 CEB).

Day 136

"Dear brothers and sisters, when troubles come your way, consider it an opportunity for great joy. For you know that when your faith is tested, your endurance has a chance to grow. So let it grow, for when your endurance is fully developed, you will be perfect and complete, needing nothing" (James 1:2–4 NLT)

Day 137

"In the Messiah, in Christ, God leads us from place to place in one perpetual victory parade. Through us, he brings knowledge of Christ. Everywhere we go, people breathe in the exquisite fragrance" (2 Corinthians 2:14 MSG).

Day 138

We all need a little spiritual refresher every so often. This is why it is important to be a part of the body of Christ.

Surround yourself with believers and allow your spirit to be refreshed through the spiritual strength of those around you.

Day 139

"Let those who plant with tears reap the harvest with joyful shouts" (Psalm 126:5 CEB).

Day 140

"You want what you don't have, so you scheme and kill to get it. You are jealous of what other have, but you can't get it, so you fight and wage war to take it away from them. Yet you don't have what you want because you don't ask God for it" (James 4:2 NLT).

Day 141

You can't make someone read the latest research, you can't make someone compassionate, and you cannot take away the arrogance and dangerous insecurities possessed by any one person.

Day 142

Embrace the moments that you find yourself on your knees with desperation. For these are the quiet moments that we may best hear His voice, because these are the moments that we are often most focused on Him.

Day 143

"He was more honored than the other members of the Thirty, though he was not one of the Three. And David made him captain of his bodyguard" (2 Samuel 23:23 NLT)

Day 144

A doctor is only as good as their mind is open.

Day 145

"But as for me, God forbid that I should boast about anything except for the cross of our Lord Jesus Christ. The world has been crucified to me through him, and I have been crucified to the world" (Galatians 6:14 CEB).

Day 146

And when we realize that we are meant for something greater, it becomes easier to wait patiently. Of course that does not mean waiting is easy; rather, it is less difficult.

Day 147

"Don't be conformed to the patterns of this world, but be transformed by the renewing of your minds so that you can figure out what God's will is—what is good and pleasing and mature" (Romans 12:2 CEB).

Day 148

Do not let your past nor present discourage you in this journey. Whatever battle you are fighting, it is transforming you into the person you are supposed to become. Use this lesson wisely so as to not have to repeat it.

Day 149

"I ask that you'll know the love of Christ that is beyond knowledge so that you will be filled entirely with the fullness of God" (Ephesians 3:19 CEB).

Day 150

Facing our fears is not always the easiest thing to do. But when we stare them straight in the eye, something remarkable happens within us. We soon find that we are greater than what we fear, because fear is nothing more than a lie—a lie used to try to prevent us from becoming what we are meant to become.

Day 151

"You are from God, little children, and you have defeated these people because the one who is in you is greater than the one who is in the world" (1 John 4:4 CEB).

Day 152

Some people want it.
Some people wish they had it.
Others go out and get it.

Day 153

"I assure you that whoever believes in me will do the works that I do. They will do even greater works than these because I am going to the Father. I will do whatever you ask for in my name, so that the Father can be glorified in the Son. When you ask me for anything in my name, I will do it" (John 14:12–14 CEB).

Day 154

There is no such thing as luck. Success comes from following God's will for your life through faith and hard work.

Day 155

"There is no fear in love, but perfect love drives out fear, because fear expects punishment. The person who is afraid has not been made perfect in love" (1 John 4:18 CEB).

Day 156

Sometimes we need to pause and evaluate who we are surrounding ourselves with. Are the people surrounding you providing you with the spiritual support that you need?

Day 157

"Let's not get tired of doing good, because in time we'll have a harvest if we don't give up" (Galatians 6:9 CEB).

Day 158

Why are you so afraid to become greater than you have ever imagined?

Day 159

"Don't speak in the ears of fools, for they will scorn your insightful words" (Proverbs 23:9 CEB).

Day 160

"The Lord isn't slow to keep his promise, as some think of slowness, but he is patient toward you, not wanting anyone to perish but all to change their hearts and lives" (2 Peter 3:9 CEB).

Day 161

When you feel that you cannot go on, when you fall to the ground, don't forget to look up. For He will be there to lift you back up onto your feet.

And as He has been this whole time, He will continue to walk beside you through all of this.

Day 162

"It is better to be a poor but wise youth than an old and foolish king who refuses all advise" (Ecclesiastes 4:13).

Day 163

For so long you have said to yourself, "I wish I had . . ." and "It would be nice if . . ." At what moment in your life will you stop simply wishing and hoping? At what moment will you decide that now is the time to become greater? At what moment will you finally realize that everything you want to do and become is within your reach?

Day 164

"For many are called, but few are chosen" (Matthew 22:14).

Day 165

"Yet what we suffer now is nothing compared to the glory he will reveal" (Romans 8:18).

Day 166

"Jesus prayed, 'Father, forgive them; they don't know what they're doing" (Luke 23:34 MSG).

Day 167

Don't you dare give up!
This is not over because you have
not crossed the finish line.
Keep going!

Day 168

Sometimes it's not about losing weight.
Sometimes it's about fighting for your life.

Day 169

Titles and ranks don't mean much if they don't have ears to listen nor minds to remain open.

Day 170

You say that you believe, but you have such fear and doubt. How then is God to fill your desires when you hold onto such things?

Day 171

And so as we start a new day, let us thank the Lord for giving us another day . . . another opportunity to pursue His will for our life. Let us be grateful for the plans that He has for us.

Day 172

As we wait for that "final destination," let us not forget how far we have come. Let us reflect upon what great success we have achieved thus far on this journey. If you feel that you have not come so far, do not be fooled, for you have grown greater and stronger than you realize.

Day 173

"You're my cave to hide in, my cliff to climb. Be my safe leader, be my true mountain guide. Free me from hidden traps; I want to hide in you. I've put my life in your hands. You won't drop me, you'll never let me down" (Psalm 31:3–5 MSG).

Day 174

You Are a Survivor.
You have decided not to be a victim anymore.
Tell your story.
It may very well make a survivor out of someone else.

Day 175

Do not be discouraged. Help is on the way.
Trust and believe in God's perfect timing.

Day 176

Sing to him with the passion that is within your soul. He will hear your song and answer it with perfect love and grace.

Day 177

"Patient endurance is what you need now, so that you will continue to do God's will. Then you will receive all that he has promised" (Hebrews 10:36).

Day 178

For I know that your patience is being tested. I know that you feel like you cannot take much more. But remember that it is just when we are about to break that the miracles begin!

Day 179

There is no circumstance that is too great for Him. Have you forgotten to truly hand yours over to Him?

Day 180

When was the last time He failed you? Never. So why would he fail you now? Wait patiently for the answer, my brothers and sisters.

Day 181

"But the one who endures to the end will be delivered" (Matthew 24:13 CEB).

Day 182

"I can endure all these things through the power of the one who gives me strength" (Philippians 4:13 CEB).

Day 183

"We're praying this so that you can live lives that are worthy of the Lord and pleasing to him in every way: by producing fruit in every good work and growing in the knowledge of God; by being strengthened through his glorious might so that you endure everything and have patience" (Colossians 1:10–11 CEB).

Day 184

"Instead, he endured the torture with honor, as if he were transformed by the fire into a life without end. He said, 'Imitate me, brothers. Don't desert your post in this contest or deny the courage we share as brothers'" (4 Maccabees 9:22–23 CEB).

Day 185

"Look at how we honor those who have practiced endurance. You have heard of the endurance of Job. And you have seen what the Lord has accomplished, for the Lord is full of compassion and mercy" (James 5:11 CEB).

Day 186

"You were called to this kind of endurance, because Christ suffered on your behalf. He left you an example so that you might follow in his footsteps" (1 Peter 2:21).

Day 187

"All people, including the ones who tortured them, were amazed at their courage and patient endurance. What's more, they caused the defeat of the tyranny that had oppressed their nation. They conquered the tyrant by their endurance. As a result, their homeland was purged of its filth through their actions" (4 Maccabees 1:11 CEB).

Day 188

"When my endurance was weakening, I remembered the Lord and my prayer came to you, to your holy temple" (Jonah 2:7 CEB).

Day 189

"Instead, make yourselves beautiful on the inside, in your hearts, with the enduring quality of a gentle, peaceful spirit. This type of beauty is very precious in God's eyes" (1 Peter 3:4 CEB).

Day 190

"The Lord proclaims: Keep your voice from crying and your eyes from weeping, because your endurance will be rewarded, declares the Lord. They will return from the land of their enemy" (Jeremiah 31:16 CEB).

Day 191

"This is why I endure everything for the sake of those who are chosen by God so that they too may experience salvation in Christ Jesus with eternal glory" (2 Timothy 2:10 CEB).

Day 192

"This calls for the endurance of the saints, who keep God's commandments and keep faith with Jesus" (Revelation 14:12 CEB).

Day 193

"Patience leads to abundant understanding,
but impatience leads to stupid mistakes"
(Proverbs 14:29 CEB).

Day 194

"Accept whatever happens to you, and be patient when you suffer humiliation" (Sirach 2:4 CEB).

Day 195

"Be strong and courageous," David said to his son Solomon. "Get to work. Don't be afraid or discouraged, because the Lord God, my God, is with you. He'll neither let you down nor leave you before all the work for the service of the Lord's temple is done" (1 Chronicles 28:20 CEB).

Day 196

"Today my complaint is again bitter; my strength is weighed down because of my groaning" (Job 23:2 CEB).

Day 197

"Pursue the Lord and his strength; seek his face always" (Psalm 105:4 CEB).

Day 198

"Because you have kept My word about patient endurance, I will also keep you from the hour of trial that is coming upon the whole world to test those who dwell on the earth" (Revelation 3:10 TLV).

Day 199

"I waited and waited and waited for God. At last he looked; finally he listened. He lifted me out of the ditch, pulled me from deep mud. He stood me up on a solid rock to make sure I wouldn't slip. He taught me how to sing the latest God-song, a praise-song to our God. More and more people are seeing this: they enter the mystery, abandoning themselves to God" (Psalm 40:1–3 MSG).

Day 200

"We do not want you to become lazy, but to be like those who believe and are patient, and so receive what God has promised" (Hebrews 6:12 GNB).

Day 201

After working so hard, we often become tired. This is true for our physical being, as well as our spiritual being. It can become easy to put off praying and saying our thanks. Let us not allow our tired spirits and physical bodies to stop us from receiving his peace and grace.

Day 202

"Wait patiently for God, don't leave the path. He'll give you your place in the sun while you watch the wicked lose it" (Psalm 37:34 MSG).

Day 203

If God led you to this road, He will continue to guide your walk. Sometimes that walk seems a little longer than we would like it to be and sometimes we may feel that others are receiving things that they do not deserve. But do not worry, for you will make it to the end with much honor and glory in His name. Those who do wrong around you will not take the lead.

Day 204

So it has been said through the spoken Word of Jesus Christ that in Him there is no fear, no measurable amount of destruction that can ever conquer your heart. In the trance of the Spirit, we find a holy place that, like no other, the chosen will enter.

So overflow your cup. Let it overflow and pour out to the masses. Your gift is a special one, so do not let it drown. Cherish all that you have been given, for it will serve you well on this earth. Embrace the heartaches, for they will build the strong walls upon the foundation of Jesus Christ.

Day 205

And so yet again we find ourselves in the presence of the Lord. What message will he bring tonight? And what is it that I am to share? It comes in the middle of me rambling on, waiting to receive.

My fear and doubt were washed away tonight as I again received the gift of tongues and translation where I receive that there is nothing like hearing the words of Jesus. As I prayed for a man who is so desperate to be in God's presence, I received that he is out there waiting as well. I continued waiting for a message to enter into my book, but did not receive anything. I wondered if I was to just share my experience of speaking in tongues and confirmation that a God fearing man is out there for me. Perhaps, this was another moment where I received one answer, while waiting for another.

Day 206

It does not matter what the spiritual warfare is.
It does not matter what the battle is.
There is only one who wins and one who is defeated.
There is no explanation needed.
You are His, and you are to be left alone.

Day 207

And as the ocean waves crash back and forth, so do the wars of this world. Do not be disheartened by what you see around you, for it is only but a false world that we are in. This is not our true dwelling place, so do not forget where you belong.

Day 208

Bring the light to me, O Lord. I want to see your face. I want to be in your presence, God. I cannot help but fall in love with you more deeply and ever so greatly.

Day 209

Lord Jesus, please do not keep your words from me. I want to continue receiving your message. Let me be your disciple. Jesus, let me hear the words that have never been spoken or written. Let me be the messenger for your spoken word. The words that only those living with you heard.

Bring me into your holy place, Father. I cannot stand what is being said, what is being spoken. Lord Jesus, we cannot believe what is being said, what is being spoken.

Day 210

How can we stop this Jesus? What is it that we can do? Is there nothing? And we understand why you do this, why you allow this, but we cannot bear this. Is there no other way?

Day 211

Bring me into your Holy place Jesus.
I so desperately want to be in your presence.
Fill me like never before.
Fill me with a greater hope, greater than ever before.
Bring me love that I have never felt before.
Bring me healing like I have never known.
Bring me someone who feels the same.
Jesus, I pray to you, expecting these things.
I thank you for these things.

Day 212

Grab onto Him tighter than ever before. Become closer to him. Do not let go. He will surely never let go of you, but holding onto Him will strengthen the bond. There will surely be a force trying to separate you. But should you stay ever so close, breast to breast, face to face, cheek to cheek, in such a tight embrace, how much more difficult it is to separate you. It is impossible. If ever one thought it were impossible for God to be separated from you, it becomes more impossible for you to fear another force. So stay as close as you can and show off your faithfulness when they arrive. They will flee. They cannot stand such words nor love.

Day 213

Doubt is a lie.
Do not be pressed by it, for it will
defeat trust if you allow it.

Day 214

Oh, how He loves you.
Do not forget this wondrous fact through your struggles.

Day 215

As we wait for His answer, the one that we truly seek, live with peace in your heart, knowing that His grace and love are truly all we need in this life.

Day 216

And as the roads become rough and difficult to travel upon, let us not forget to look to the side, for sometimes he gives us a way out, but we pass it by. Sometimes He wants us to stay the road, but sometimes He allows us a different path to take.

Day 217

What is the fire that He has given you?
There is indeed a passion that He has
placed within your heart.
This is what you are to pursue. Do not ignore it.

Day 218

Patient endurance for a relationship may surely be a tough one. Some may pray for their significant other to find the Lord while others seek a godly partner. Whatever your relationship status, let us not forget that when the timing is right, the relationship will fall ever so perfectly into place.

Day 219

And when the words come, all will know that Jesus Christ is King. These are the words that are to be remembered. For there is no other who can provide such power and restoration to your life.

Day 220

From the beginning, you were already created.
Your purpose was already written in stone.
So you see, there is nothing that is a surprise
to God, though it may be a surprise to us.

Day 221

Let us follow the path that he has laid out for us. When we stray, he will guide us back to our road. The detours that we take ourselves have been accounted for, and He will use them for our benefit. This is not to say that we should stray. But should it happen, do not be afraid of your doings. They will be turned around and made into God's perfect timing.

Day 222

Once you decide to follow the ways of the Lord Jesus Christ, something wondrous will occur in your life. There are no words to describe the power that is brought into your spirit and into your days. Rather it can only be understood by each one of us experiencing these things that only He can provide.

Day 223

Whatever your physical body is telling you, your spirit knows something greater. The sickness, the pains, and these feelings that you experience are nothing compared to the amazing joy that is brought by the spirit. Surrender all to Him, and He will bring peace and joy into your soul.

Day 224

Sometimes the test of love is patience.

Day 225

Lord Jesus, we thank you for the gift of love that You have brought upon us. You have filled our hearts with something so wondrous, and we are so grateful.

Day 226

After searching, seeking, and praying, the two hearts shall meet and become one.

Day 227

For this is no ordinary love, the love of the Savior. This love is itself a miracle. For how could one man endure such a torturous death in the name of love?

Day 228

In this journey, persistence may be the simple answer. The difficult answer, however, is patience.

Day 229

Oh, to be struck by the Holy Spirit and receive such wondrous gifts. How we wait patiently to receive such things. When we should be so blessed, this sacred gift will be revealed.

Day 230

The longing of your heart's desire will
be satisfied in God's time.

Day 231

Oh, how long must we wait to receive the answer to our quest? Though I am not sure what battle you are fighting or what path you are struggling to journey upon, I do know one thing. I know that God is faithful and that He will never fail you nor let you down. While we can become impatient and confused along this journey, we must always remember that His timing and his reasons are different from what we can comprehend.

Day 232

Sing his praises all of your days. Even on the rainy and stormy days, sing His praise. It will call out the light and allow His grace to shine through the storm.

Day 233

Oh, how love is worth waiting for. Though sometimes we must wait to find that "perfect love," when the time comes, it is a love so worth the wait.

Day 234

Gracious endurance endures all things.
As you face this hardship head-on, do it with grace.
Though it may take all that you have, you
will receive abundance in return.

Day 235

Lord Jesus, fill me up tonight. Strike my soul with Your spirit so that my heart will understand Your wonder. Fill my spirit with Your Word. Your Word so true, and Your Word so firm. Lord Jesus, bring me into the place where only You belong. I so desperately seek You tonight, Jesus.

Day 236

This is my prayer today. As we walk through the battles of the everyday, let us feel Your presence in our hearts and in our souls. Lord God, Father, we need You, and we know that You are with us each day. Though we may not always feel Your presence, we know that You bless us each one of our days. We thank You for such love.

Day 237

Lord Jesus, be with me today as I face this battle face to face. I need You ever so greatly today, my Father, my God. I trust You, and I thank You for all that You do.

Day 238

Lord Jesus, I cannot understand what is happening. Please bring an understanding and peace into my heart and soul so that I may proceed further. This struggle is so hard and I don't know where else to turn. So I turn to You, the only one who can truly help me.

Day 239

Mighty God, Your power is so wondrous. I come to You today with such gratitude in my heart. I thank You for helping me in this test. I thank You for allowing me this opportunity to grow greater in my relationship with You. I thank You for allowing me the opportunity to grow my trust in You. Thank You for loving me so much and for entrusting me with such a duty here on this earth.

Day 240

Father, I thank You for the chains that You have removed from my spirit. My heart and soul were tormented, but not as much as my spirit. It is because of Your love and grace that I have been saved and that my spirit can sing ever so freely. Because of this, my heart and my soul may also sing a great song. Thank You, Lord Jesus, for Your sacrifice and for Your never-ending grace.

Day 241

Jesus, I come to you tonight with such thanksgiving and gratitude in my heart. I know that You want only the best for me. I know that your timing is not my timing, and how grateful I am that this is so. For your timing is perfect always.

Day 242

I welcome failure because it allows me the opportunity to try again with greater knowledge. I welcome a broken heart because it gives me an opportunity to build a stronger one. I welcome every trial because I know that they serve a greater purpose for my life. I welcome the doubters because they give me a chance to prove my strength to myself, not to them. I welcome all the hardships and trials because without them, who would I be besides skin and bones? Bring on the heartache, bring on the hurt, bring on the failures. These are the tools needed to become the person I am to become.

Day 243

Sometimes we may feel as though we have run out of patience; we become tired of waiting and wonder what God is truly thinking. We need to still remember that He continues to prepare our hearts.

So even when we think we cannot take another moment of waiting, He is training our hearts, our minds, and our spirits.

Remain strong in your journey.

The final destination may not be as far away as you think.

Day 244

Fear not, for all things will fall into place in just the exact way they are meant to fall.

Day 245

Be patient for love.
Do not expect anything, yet rather embrace
every moment that you are given.

Day 246

Love works through actions, not just through the spoken word. For what are words when there is no action to accompany them?

Day 247

The patient heart may often wander after a period of waiting. Let us catch ourselves during these desert moments and bring our feet back to where they belong. Let our hearts be brought back to the Spirit, where it belongs.

Day 248

So while you wait patiently, reflect upon the moments that have led you to this place. What lessons have you learned thus far that can help you with this next step? Surely, you have been equipped for these next moments.

Day 249

The patient heart waits without angst. It waits with love, peace, comfort, reassurance, and a hope and joy for what is to come.

Day 250

Find yourself surrounded by those who are filled with patience. For when you surround yourself with such people, you too will experience the peace that is received. Should you find yourself surrounded by those lacking patience, you may then also find yourself surrounded by anxiety, frustration, and anger.

Day 251

Sometimes we may feel that life throws
us unreasonable circumstances.
Let us be patient as we await for the purpose
and the meaning of these trying times.

Day 252

Lord Jesus, change my heart, O God. My heart has been emptied of love and patience. I have allowed myself to be consumed with anxiety, frustration, and doubt. Jesus, I ask you in this moment to redesign my heart. Let others see this reformation through each encounter. Lord God, I pray in this moment for understanding so that I may avoid such emptying in the times to come. Jesus, help keep me patient, kind, loving, and filled with You. I pray these things in Your holy name.

Day 253

Father, forgive me for my wandering heart. I have been impatient with this life and have tried to find comfort in others rather than in You. Lord, help me with my endurance to pursue You and You alone. Help keep me away from the temptations of this world. Let me find my peace in You.

Day 254

Our hearts seek so desperately to find answers to our questions. Let us be quiet and listen for the Lord's answer. Sometimes it takes some time to hear His words, but let us not stop our seeking for His and only His response.

Day 255

We tend to bring on the pains of this life ourselves. God has the power to turn these pains into lessons of patience and endurance. He turns our mistakes into learning experiences. If you feel that you have made a mistake, fear not, for the Lord our God will turn it around for your benefit.

Day 256

Do not rush into or out of a circumstance.
Teach yourself how to be patient with whatever you
are going through and with whomever you are with.
You will gain strength in patience.

Day 257

In wandering through the darkness, there will soon be return of the light.

Day 258

In the confusion of the moment, hold on to what you know to be true.

Day 259

Father God, I thank You for restoring my sight, for I became blind for a while, but now I can see again. You are ever faithful.

Day 260

Holy Spirit, I thank You for filling me with Your presence. Though my spirit remained connected, my soul had strayed. Thank You for showing me Your love once again. Thank You for always welcoming me back with open arms. Though I do not deserve Your grace, you give it so freely.

Day 261

Jesus, you have taken my heartache and burdens away. I do not know what led me to stray from Your holy presence. All that matters is that I have returned to seek You. And as You always do, You have welcomed me with the same love and grace that has never changed. Despite all that I have done, I know that I can always return to You, for your love is truly unconditional. Your love is truly like no other.

Day 262

"Then Haggai, the LORD's messenger, gave the people this message from the Lord: 'I am with you, says the Lord!'" (Haggai 1:13.)

Day 263

When we feel the struggle has only become more difficult, when things seem to be falling apart, and perhaps even come to a halt, perhaps that is God forcing us to stop what we are doing so that we can refocus on what is the most important: Him.

Once your focus has been restored and your relationship reestablished, then He can restart your path.

Day 264

You are not the only one experiencing such despair, frustration, anxiety, and stress. Today, try to help encourage someone else who is facing a struggle in their own life. Doing this allows us to take the focus off our own situation and help someone out in their time of need.

Day 265

When seeking advice from those around you, be sure that you select those of strong Christian faith who will provide objective guidance based upon biblical scriptures.

Day 266

Whatever it is that you are allowing to cause stress in your life, just stop here in this moment. Is this something you can control? If yes, then do something about it. Is it something that you cannot control? If your answer is yes to this question, then perhaps you must reevaluate how you are approaching this issue, because stress is most surely not a productive solution.

Day 267

Sometimes life does not offer us the things that we desire—or when we desire them. Sometimes we are pushed farther than what we feel we can hold on to. But what will be just simply will be. Whether we are working on making something happen, or have lost all possible control, what is meant to be will be. So continue to do your best at growing, enduring, and being patient. But do not be discouraged if a sudden detour is placed in front of you.

Day 268

In the larger picture that is life, what is really important to you? Perhaps write these things down, and when a thing creates stress and uneasiness, go back to the list of "things important in this life." Does this new "thing" fit into this list somewhere? If it does not, then it does not deserve such passionate emotion.

Day 269

As you press on throughout your struggle, do not forget about those around you. Allow others to be there for you. And allow yourself to be there for them as well.

Day 270

As you press on, you continue to learn about yourself. And as you continue to do so, you may realize various things about the relationships you maintain in your life—for example, which ones do you feel you need to work on more, which ones do you need to let go of? And regardless of the answers to the various questions you begin to ask yourself, you may be faced with one question in particular that may require further action. Today you are asked this question: would you be okay with the way you left each conversation with each person in your life if you found out they were no longer here?

Day 271

I am not sure upon which road you are traveling. And I am not sure what it is that you are facing. But if you are in a place where you find yourself feeling lost, perhaps now is the moment when you are not actually lost. Rather, perhaps now you stand in a place where God has invited only you. It is a place that you must be in order to understand something greater. Perhaps other avenues of learning have proven to be unsuccessful and you have now been led to this place. It might be painful. It might be confusing. It may feel lonely. You may feel as though so much is now uncertain.

In the moments when you feel such things, I again ask you to stop in the moment. Stop and remember who it is that you have trusted with your life. So while you may feel lost, you are not. You may not be able to see an inch through the fog in front of you or beyond the desert's horizon, but He is able. He knows exactly what is beyond what you cannot see.

Day 272

Continue to pursue all that your heart desires. Never put your passions aside.

Day 273

You are worth every wonderful thing. So never at any moment settle for even a little bit less than wonderful.

Day 274

A letter of gratitude:

So the past few months of my life have been interesting. While some events have brought a great deal of pain and confusion, I have been met with some pretty awesome things too; from connecting with remarkable family members, to reconnecting with an old friend, to starting something new on the other side of the country.

For so long, I always had specific goals set in my mind, and I always had a plan on how to reach each one of those goals, never doubting getting to the finish line and beyond.

Generally speaking, for most things in life, there is a classic road to take for various goals or certain sequential steps/events that need to happen in order to reach a final endpoint. (If you want to be a doctor, for example, you have to go through four years of undergrad while spreading yourself thin trying to be superhuman to get into medical school so you can then work even harder for another four years to get a residency, then even more so for the next three-plus years to really understand medicine and possibly gain an attending position, etc. Okay, so maybe not the most basic example I could have used.)

Anyway, away from my digression.

What these past months have shown me is that while most people may follow the "standard path," some of us are taken on a more "self-reflecting" road. I have no true reasoning for such a thing that continues to test one's patience, endurance, and even faith. Such an unconventional journey really tests a person, outside of one's understanding, while simultaneously pushing them beyond the limits they thought they could handle. Why some get to be chosen to go down this road, as opposed to the less hazardous road, well, I have no idea.

Recent life events have not simply "allowed" me to reevaluate (my) life, but they have absolutely forced me to do so. Looking back at the past handful-plus years, would I have done things differently? Well, I could say yes, but I would surely always wonder "what if" and have a great deal of regret for not pursuing the things of my heart's desire.

And surely everyone knows that each person and event in our lives shapes us in some way. Without the more trying times, we would not truly know our own strength and capabilities. Without difficult and failed relationships, we would not appreciate the good ones. And for the amazing times and remarkable people—they allow us to see the genuine beauty in life. And this is where I am today, genuinely filled with gratitude for the people who have reminded me of the greater things that simply are.

My family, for one, is really absolutely remarkable. Everyone should be so blessed to have a family like the one that I have. From my parents and sister, to aunts, uncles, and grandparents, it's incredible at how blessed I am with the family I have been given.

I have also been shown true friendship, and my favorite kind of friendships are the ones that pick up right where you left off despite the amount of time that has lapsed from the last time you spoke. I have been blessed with some of those, and I value them tremendously.

And really, while I have absolutely no idea what is going to happen next in my life, there are a few things that I do know.

I am grateful for everyone who has come into my life. Each person has done something for me in some way, knowingly or not. And if you're reading this, then it means that you are one of those people. Honestly.

Some have proven to be a missing piece to a shattered past and have allowed me to realize that some passions never really die. Some have shown me that even in the name of love, you must always remain true to the passions of your spirit and soul. Others have shown gestures of kindness and generosity and have demonstrated true sincerity while showing me the type of person I want to be and the type of people I want to be surrounded by. Some have been extraordinarily empowering.

Because of those in my life, I also now know that I love a great Moscato wine and brie. Blues is the music of my soul, and Hillsong represents the music of my spirit. I am a beach girl for sure, and I could never settle too far from the ocean! The passion for playing music still circulates throughout my blood, and I will not let it succumb to Virchow's triad. And of course, there's Krav Maga.

Ultimately, what I have been led to question is this: If everything that you have relentlessly worked for and everything you ever dreamed of were completely ripped away from reality, what would you find yourself left with? Would you even know the reality of who you are? What would you do next? Who would you turn to? And who would be there?

Day 275

And so I say again, patient endurance for a relationship may surely be a tough one. Perhaps it is the relationship with a friend or family member that you desire to be different. You must remember that you can only change yourself and your own behaviors. Be kind and act with love. Pray for God to move in such a way that your relationship will no longer produce stress or strain; rather, may it enable peace and acceptance.

Day 276

Remember that your actions will always speak louder than your words and that words can leave irremovable scars.

Day 277

In this life, you will never know the true impact that you have had on others. You will never know to what depth you have moved someone's soul. So never discount your worth. You are valued at a far greater price than you could truly ever imagine.

Day 278

These moments that you have been forced to go through will not only build and strengthen you; they will create the opportunity to help others who will face similar—if not the same—trials.

Day 279

Strengthen yourself so that you may be able to help strengthen others.

Day 280

When we meet a person, we may only be able to gauge their previous actions by trusting their words. Moving forward, we may only be able to trust their words by observing their actions.

Day 281

How tired are you? Are you overwhelmingly exhausted? If your answer is yes, then I suggest that you stop resisting God's will for your life.

Day 282

It cannot be repeated enough, because we as people tend to think that we messed everything up. However, not only will God redirect your life after you have wandered off path, but he will allow your additional journey to become an additional tool for your great purpose.

Day 283

If each door seems to be shutting in your face or simply does not open at all, it is because none of those doors are yours to go through.

Day 284

Surrender. Submit. Trust. Believe. Listen. Follow. Go. And be grateful for the unknown that is to come. For when you surrender, submit, trust, believe, listen, follow, and go, you know that the unknown is going to be far greater than anything you could have ever imagined.

Day 285

When you drop all the useless baggage that you have carried for so long and decide to walk the road that God has made for you, rather than the one you have tried to make for yourself, a few things will begin to happen. For example, you will soon approach doors that you will not need to knock on. When you walk up to them, they will be opened for you.

Day 286

To satisfy your soul, listen to your spirit, for your spirit is being called by the Spirit. When you submit to the calling, you can then start to truly live your purpose. You will only gain true understanding of this feeling when this is done.

Day 287

Some things are just out of our control. All we can do is the best that we can and believe that everything will be okay. Having faith in Christ to get us through those times is sometimes all we can do, and really, that's all we need. Because He will come through in His timing.

Day 288

If there is something that you dream of doing but you are doubtful in your ability or are too afraid, do it anyway. If there is a place you want to go to, go there. If you feel a strong calling, answer it. Your life will start to make sense when you respond obediently to God's direction.

Day 289

If someone literally gave me a million dollars, there would still not be any comparison to the gift that is the opportunity to live the life that I have been given.

Day 290

You will find yourself in amazement and surrounded by wonder. What you never could have even imagined to dream about will be given to you as opportunities to take and experience.

Day 291

I am waiting for your next move, God. And I must be honest, though I have grown in You and I trust on most days, I still find myself afraid sometimes. I know that You have Your plan in mind and that I just need to remember how You always come through. I think that I just need to feel Your comfort just a little extra tonight. I do not want to be persuaded by the enemy and believe his lies. So please just come. Surround me tonight and let me feel secure in You.

Day 292

I have responded to Your call and followed Your voice. I have gone to the place You have asked, and I will remain in this place until You send me to the next place.

Day 293

I do not know your plan, but I believe that it is a great one. So if I have to wait even a little bit more, then that I will do.

Day 294

It truly is a continual test of patience, this life. But imagine what will happen when you surrender to becoming patient. You will no longer be anxious.

I envision God to be the epitome of *relaxed* even in guiding us through each step of our lives. I imagine that He just gently guides us with his hands, wanting us to be as stressless as Him.

Day 295

You will always be thrown a distraction. Even when you follow the path made specifically for your life, distractions will come. Especially when you follow the path made specifically for your life, distractions will come.

Stay focused on the Lord. Redirect your eyes to him. Remember why you have returned to his call for your life. There is nothing worth getting off God's purposely created road for your life. Nothing.

Day 296

Do not let your faith guide only your thoughts but your actions as well. For while your thoughts and beliefs may reflect your faith, people do not reside within your mind.

When you act upon your faith, you demonstrate something greater than yourself. And as a follower of Christ, your faithful actions will be of trust and love.

Day 297

And so I ask you again, how much have you surrendered to God? Nothing, a little, some, much, most, almost everything, or everything completely?

PS: From "almost everything" to "everything completely," there is quite a remarkable difference.

Day 298

Never aim lower than the unimaginable.

Day 299

For never will there be a day when you are not protected.

Day 300

Dream of the impossible.
Receive the perceived impossible.
Receive unimagined possibilities.

Day 301

You have weaknesses. Everyone does.
It is your weakness that will be used
to prove that miracles occur.
Your weakness will be used to show just
how possible every single thing is when
you have God playing on your team.

Day 302

One day, you will stop in the very moment that you are in. You will pause and examine your surroundings. You will find yourself existing among the perceived impossibilities of your life. You will realize that you have been chosen. You will realize that you have been surrounded with an extremely rare protection throughout the relentless struggles that you have battled. Though you may not understand the true significance of it all, in that very moment, you will know that your journey is only then really just beginning.

Day 303

For today is here. Tomorrow is a gift. Believe in the unseen. Keep your eyes Arise. Pursuit. Unrelenting pursuit. The challenge may be great, but the purpose is far greater. There will be haters, liars, and deceivers, but continue on. Focus not on them or other obstacles. Rather, focus on why you have returned to this place and who it is who brought you here from the start.

Day 304

Stop thinking that it cannot be done.
Stop thinking that it is impossible.

Day 305

Your trials are your training for the purpose that God has designated for only you.

Day 306

While you are being trained and deeply conditioned, so are your teammates—that is, those who will work with you in the field of your life's purpose are also being trained. When God has deemed it time for you all to come together, you will find yourself being introduced to one amazing human after the other. They will likely also be followers of Christ. They will be courageous. They will have been well trained, and they will be ready to join together to fulfill God's will.

Day 307

Know the story before you judge someone from their title alone.

Day 308

While knowledge may be power, ignorance of those who hold a position of power can prove devastating to those with the power of knowledge.

Day 309

Never be so quick to assume that one's appearance is that person's entire reality.

Day 310

Refocus. Where did your joy go? Did you forget where you found your joy? Are you staying in His Word? Are you in it enough? Correct this accordingly.

Day 311

Be okay with *just* you and God in this situation and in every situation. Anyone else who supports you is a bonus and an extra gift. But be okay with God being the only one in this with you.

Day 312

Sometimes you need to let it out. Let out your frustration, your heartache, your confusion. Cry it out. Scream it out. Heavy-bag it out.

Day 313

I relocated on faith. Without a job or a place to live, I moved on faith. Things immediately began to fall into place. Then I found myself allowing walls to rise up and stand between me and my relationship with God. After allowing these walls to rise, I was pulled back into His Word and realized that I had lost my joy, and had even gained a great deal of stress and angst during this separation period. I again made a decision that I needed to stay connected to Christ. So whatever was taking away my worship time was itself taken out of my life. I needed to be drawn back to Him. He was the reason I relocated. I felt called to do so. And even though I moved in faith, I still was faced with a battle of staying focused on Him.

Day 314

Charles Nieman has a series called *Alpha and Omega*. If you needed this spiritual motivation book, then I recommend you watch this series by Charles Nieman. It put so much into perspective and is still the best message that I have personally heard to date.

Day 315

"You intended to harm me, but God intended it all for good. He brought me to this position so I could save the lives of many people" (Genesis 50:20).

Day 316

God, take this anger from me, please. My spirit clings to you still, but my flesh still is having a hard time waiting for my purpose. I thought that I knew what you wanted for my life. But I have become so lost and confused. The road that I thought you had destined for me turned out to be a far different one than I ever expected. God, I know that everything is in your timing. I need your help now, because I feel so defeated. I keep running into one closed door after the other. Please give me a clear, open door, God. I am on my knees.

Day 317

Just put everything on hold for at least an hour today. Whatever you "just have to get done" is not as important as needing to get your Jesus time done. Pause for a brief period of your day to submerge into His Word. You will be renewed.

Day 318

"Then the Lord spoke to Jonah a second time. Get up and go to the great city of Neneveh, and deliver the message I have given you" (Jonah 3:1–2).

Day 319

"The Lord replied, 'Is it right for you to be angry about this?'" (Jonah 4:4).

Day 320

"I know all the things you do, and I have opened a door for you that no one can close. You have little strength, yet you obeyed my word and did not deny me" (Revelation 3:8).

Day 321

"Write this letter to the angel of the church in Philadelphia. This is the message from the one who is holy and true, the one who has the key of David. What he opens, no one can close; and what he closes, no one can open" (Revelation 3:7).

Day 322

"I am the Alpha and the Omega—the beginning and the end," says the Lord God. "I am the one who is, who always was, and who is still to come—the Almighty One" (Revelation 1:8).

Day 323

"Do not despise these small beginnings, for the Lord rejoices to see the work begin, to see the plumb line in Zerubbabel's hand" (Zechariah 4:10).

Day 324

"This is what the Lord of Heaven's Armies says: All this may seem impossible to you now, a small remnant of God's people. But is it impossible for me? Says the Lord of Heaven's Armies" (Zechariah 8:6).

Day 325

"Among the other nations, Judah and Israel became symbols of a cursed nation. But no longer! Now I will rescue you and make you both a symbol and a source of blessing. So don't be afraid. Be strong, and get on with rebuilding the temple" (Zechariah 8:13).

Day 326

"This is what the Lord of Heaven's Armies says: Be strong and finish the task! Ever since the laying of the foundation of the Temple of the Lord of Heaven's Armies, you have heard what the prophets have been saying about completing the building" (Zechariah 8:9).

Day 327

So the truth is this: most people that you will encounter will never know your whole story. Most of them do not need to know it because they likely would still not understand it. It is not your responsibility to explain why you are the way you are to those who dare not try to understand.

Day 328

I know that things can get overwhelmingly frustrating. I know that circumstances can be so puzzling. You need to cling to hope in Him. Cling to a great trust in Him.

Day 329

And so again I say, "Keep fighting! Keep fighting!"

Day 330

This is not the end! He overcame so that you could too!

Day 331

"I am worn out waiting for your rescue, but I have put my hope in your word. My eyes are straining to see your promises come true. When will you comfort me?" (Psalm 119:81–82).

Day 332

"Your laws are my treasure; they are my heart's delight. I am determined to keep your decrees to the very end" (Psalm 119:111–112).

Day 333

"You made me; you created me. Now give me the sense to follow your commands" (Psalm 119:73).

Day 334

"He will not let you stumble; the one who watches over you will not slumber" (Psalm 121:3).

Day 335

"The Lord himself watches over you! The Lord stands beside you as your protective shade" (Psalm 121:5).

Day 336

"Those who trust in the Lord are as secure as Mount Zion; they will not be defeated but will endure forever. Just as the mountains surround Jerusalem, so the Lord surrounds his people, both now and forever" (Psalm 125:1–2).

Day 337

"Teach me to do your will, for you are my God. May your gracious Spirit lead me forward on a firm footing" (Psalm 143:10).

Day 338

So I don't know, but you might as well blindfold me, spin me around, and then tell me to just walk, because at this point, I have no idea which direction I am going. I cannot see where I am going, and I have no idea what is in front of me.

All that I do know is that I have come to the point where I just say, "Lead me, God. Wherever You want me to go, that is where I will go. Whatever obstacles await me, I know you will bring me through them. I know that I will get tired, but I know that you will give me rest." So I walk blindfolded.

Day 339

You know, God doesn't mess around. Everything that He gives you, He gives you for a purpose. You have been given your own personal toolbox—your own, very personal, divine toolbox made specifically for you by Him.

Use everything that He has given you. This includes the lessons that you learn from your trials. If you do not acquire the lesson, you shall repeat it until you finally acquire that "tool" that you will need for the next lesson.

Day 340

I have realized that when you are given a purpose, you will seek its fulfillment until your soul is satisfied. I have felt called to serve others and protect their health for a few decades now. When I could not afford to finish my last semester of medical school, I was shown how to serve and protect others at a different level and I have now chosen to do so.

So perhaps what you thought was your definite endpoint was a major learning experience for your true endpoint. Perhaps you will even return to that place. However, it becomes important to be open to change and to allow for new opportunities.

Day 341

"Don't be intimidated in any way by your enemies. This will be a sign to them that they are going to be destroyed, but that you are going to be saved, even by God himself" (Philippians 1:28).

Day 342

"I want to know Christ and experience the mighty power that raised him from the dead. I want to suffer with him, sharing in his death, so that one way or another I will experience the resurrection from the dead!" (Philippians 3:10–11).

Day 343

It's really rather fascinating at how the light makes the darkness go wild. Remove the light, and the darkness has nothing to fear.

Day 344

When I was sick, I had a totally brain-fog-free day. The only way I could explain how I felt was, when the storm clouds divide, the rays that shine through do so with the intense velocity of the most powerful of waterfalls.

There is a fellow at the hospital whose everyday cognition is what mine is on a clear cognition day. I think I see why I have not been allowed to have such train of thought every single day. Humility. Humility and then being incredibly appreciative of the days when my brain functions so well. And this statement will sound silly, but I see the impact of having such a great mind every single day. It does not allow for one to think that he or she needs anyone or anything else besides themselves.

Day 345

"So be strong and courageous, all you who put your hope in the Lord!" (Psalm 31:24).

Day 346

Set a goal. Stare it down every day. Claim it to be true.

Day 347

There is fight in your spirit even if you cannot feel it in your body or soul. In the lowest of moments, in the saddest times within your trials, you can rely on that deep-routed fight inside of you. It is the supernatural determination to not give up.

Day 348

In your journey, you may need to remember that some minds have been closed for so long that they have sealed themselves shut. Only God knows how to get those things open again.

Day 349

"You have already been pruned and purified by the message I have given you" (John 15:3).

Day 350

"You didn't choose me. I chose you. I appointed you to go and produce lasting fruit, so that the Father will give you whatever you ask for, using my name" (John 15:16).

Day 351

Ignorance and arrogance of those with the most power is an incredibly dangerous thing.

Day 352

"Now all glory to God, who is able, through his mighty power at work within us, to accomplish infinitely more than we might ask or think" (Ephesians 3:20).

Day 353

Not even a year ago, I decided that I needed to move back to Baltimore. I didn't have a job to arrive to nor a place to call my own. All that I knew was that I had to stop ignoring that gut feeling of needing to be in Baltimore. I just thought of all the opportunities I have been given because of that one decision.

Wow, there are so many awesome things that I'm not sure I can list them all, but some of the topics range from getting a job at Johns Hopkins, interviewing for the Dr. Oz show, getting acquainted with some phenomenal Air Force officers, working with the health department to improve HIV surveillance, prevention, and treatment rates . . . The list goes on, but I of course need to mention that I have met *so many* incredible people that I would not have otherwise *ever* met.

So my point here is this: if you feel that you are being pulled to do something or go somewhere, freaking do it. You don't have to know how everything will work out when you get there. You just have to go where you are being called, and amazing friends will be there for you, and ridiculous opportunities will be placed at your feet while you meet some of the most wonderful people around. So do that thing, move to that place, and have faith. Everything else will fall into place.

Day 354

"Look, I am coming soon, bringing my reward with me to repay all people according to their deeds. I am the Alpha and the Omega, the First and the Last, the Beginning and the End" (Revelation 22:12–13).

Day 355

"So he took me in the Spirit to a great, high mountain and he showed me the holy city, Jerusalem, descending out of heaven from God" (Revelation 21:10).

Day 356

For over a year and a half, my heart has been continually broken since losing money to finish medical school. The further out that I get, the more frequent my heart breaks.

Almost daily, I walk the halls of the number 3 hospital in the country, first walking by the magnificent Jesus statue under the dome of the original JHH. When I lost my medical school funding, I was so blessed to have been accepted into the number 1 school for public health, where I have been able to obtain funding as a part-time student.

On the bus to and from school, I hear premed students talking about the MCAT and med school applications while current medical students talk about rotations and board exams. Early on, it did not bother me as much. However, I now find myself fighting back tears when I hear these conversations. Seeing patients and physicians in the hospital forces me to fight back tears. However, I am still drawn to walk those halls. That is where I feel I belong.

I get frustrated when students appear to show no deep understanding or appreciation for their current opportunity to become physicians.

Over the past year, I have felt myself fade. I had a hope that $40K would somehow be gifted to me in some new miracle so that I could finish my medical degree. However, as time continues on, I admit that I have never been so confused. What is the meaning of all this? Sometimes I feel as though I am being taunted, watching these people who do not seem to understand the depth of the impact that they hold on the lives of so many.

I have lost so much fire over the past year. I admit that I have lost a lot of hope. I have lost a sense of purpose here. I received an incredible miracle when I was accepted into Johns Hopkins. What am I supposed to do with this? Do I go into public health? If I do, how will I pay off $400K in student debt? Do I join the military as a public health officer? Will that be enough? What about a combat medic? Would they even take me?

It seems as though everyone else around me has a reachable goal, something that I once thought that I had. I do know that there is a far greater picture to all this. Being welcomed into a phenomenal group of compassionate people at the Baltimore City Health Department and the Johns Hopkins Center for Child and Community Health Research has showed me that genuinely remarkable people still do exist. A recent site visit from the CDC allowed me to see a piece of a greater picture. And what I took away is that I most surely have no idea what is going on, but there has to be a reason for all this chaos.

There has to be a reason why, although going to an overseas medical school and not being able to finish, I was accepted into the number-one school for public health, where I can concentrate my degree on my passion of infectious diseases.

I had nearly given up pushing and fighting until that CDC visit last week and then witnessing another conversation across from me on the bus today. While I felt my heart break once more and fought back tears, something reignited within me.

When I got home, I took out a board review book and began making flash cards, the way I aced organic chemistry II. Since I am concentrating my Hopkins degree on infectious diseases, I thought that would be a good place to start reviewing.

So I do not know when I will be given the opportunity to finish my medical degree, but I have made at least one single decision—that when that moment comes, I will be prepared to jump right back in and ace my step 2 and 3 exams. Until then, I will take in what I can from my experience at this remarkable place. Hopkins has been an absolute blessing, and I do know that this rich experience is all for a greater purpose than I can see.

Day 357

Do you have a theme song or general soundtrack? If you do not listen to Christian music, I highly recommend it. There is something about music that does indeed feed both the soul and spirit. Over the years, many Christian artists have kept me connected to God when I was so greatly spiritually wounded. I am grateful for the bands, and their families, who have sacrificed so much to serve God and spread His Word around the globe.

Day 358

It is not our job to understand.
It is our job just to trust.

Day 359

Find a way to stay inspired. Even if it is something small, hold on to whatever will keep you moving forward. And keep that with you as you continue on. For me, this has been Jesus Christ. When you get tired or forget why you have kept going this long, look at your inspiration . . . and hey, guess what . . . yup, incoming cheesy line here: your own inspiration might be yourself. Accept the possibility of the impossible. Reject the idea that you have lost. Accept the fact that you are different, because you are stronger than most. Deny the thought in your mind that you are not good enough.

If you have a passion that stirs within you, if you have a dream that never fades, that is yours to work for. That is yours to live for. You are to never accept an apparent dead end. You must, perhaps, travel through fresh sand. And it is then that you will find how warriors and overcomers are made. It is the strenuous path, which no other has traveled upon. It is yours to walk. It is yours to endure through. You must continue on, for your destiny awaits at the end of this training.

Day 360

There will always be a spiritual battle raging on. The closer that you get to God, the greater the warfare that you will likely experience. Recognize it to be as such. And remember to declare who it is that you belong to.

Say it out loud, "I am a child of God. Jesus is my rock and my foundation. I am His, and He is mine. No evil shall ever win with Jesus as my rock and salvation."

Day 361

It is not over until He declares that it is, not when you fear that it is. Keep going.

Day 362

When you think you cannot feel him and you feel perhaps less than significant, He will use the light that is within you to shine to someone else. While you may not feel strong in the spirit, you still remain filled with the Holy Spirit. And God will use you to remind other believers that He still lives. He will continue to do the unexpected. So expect the unexpected in the most spectacular ways. And expect Him to use you when you don't expect it at all.

Day 363

We must stop and request to see others as Christ sees them. We must ask for help to love them in the way that Christ loves them, in the same way that Christ loves us.

Let us also ask to show the patience, kindness, and understanding of Christ to those around us. Let us ask Him for these things, not only to change ourselves, but to truly represent Him.

When He is truly represented here on earth, more lives will be changed for the far greater in an immeasurable way.

Day 364

There will always be a challenge to face. It is simply a part of this life. We must be continually challenged so that we may continually grow. And while we may not understand why we are faced against giants, we need to trust that God has a great plan for it all. It is not always easy, and it sometimes feels downright impossible.

In these moments, let us be surrounded with others who can help guide our eyes back to where our hope is found. When we feel that we have lost our ability to be patient and endure, let us see the help that He sends us here on earth. When we cannot feel Him, let us know that He is here and that He is still working in our lives.

Day 365

Every trial that you have faced has led you to this moment. You have made it to this very moment because you have endured every other trial to date. Have faith that you will make it through this one as well.

I do not know what you are facing. I do not know how impossible it seems to get through this time. But I do know that doing the seemingly impossible is what God specializes in.

So have faith in the mystery. Have faith in the frustration. Have faith in this trial.

Trust and Believe.

Be patient and endure on, my brothers and sisters in Christ. And never stop enduring until He declares that His will for your life has been completed and you are called home.

About the Author

Jennifer Le Blanc was born and raised in South Florida. She obtained her undergraduate degree in molecular biology and microbiology from the University of Central Florida and a master's degree in clinical nutrition from New York Institute of Technology. While working on her master's degree, Jennifer was also working on obtaining her medical degree. After three and a half years of medical school, life threw her for a significant detour. She was no longer able to complete the last twenty-one weeks of her MD. At just about the same time, she was given the opportunity to obtain a master of public health degree from The Johns Hopkins Bloomberg School of Public Health. Johns Hopkins truly introduced Jennifer to the field of public health. It was there that she discovered how she could apply her passions for infectious diseases and fighting human trafficking on a larger scale. She also found a passion for epidemiology and disaster preparedness. Jennifer has always considered her time at Hopkins a miracle. She is still unsure of God's ultimate plan for her life, but she has learned to just go with whatever He gives her.

CPSIA information can be obtained
at www.ICGtesting.com
Printed in the USA
BVHW042115180523
664439BV00005B/21

9 781643 494890